T0147170

The Spirit Washing Over Me

By Candise M. B. Heinlein

Illustrations by Phillip C. Heinlein
and Candise M. B. Heinlein

WESTBOW
PRESS°
A DIVISION OF THOMAS NELSON
& ZONDERVAN

WestBow Press books may be ordered through booksellers or by contacting:

WestBow Press
A Division of Thomas Nelson & Zondervan
1663 Liberty Drive
Bloomington, IN 47403
www.westbowpress.com
1 (866) 928-1240

Because of the dynamic nature of the Internet, any web addresses or
links contained in this book may have changed since publication and
may no longer be valid. The views expressed in this work are solely those
of the author and do not necessarily reflect the views of the publisher,
and the publisher hereby disclaims any responsibility for them.

Any people depicted in stock imagery provided by Getty Images are
models, and such images are being used for illustrative purposes only.
Certain stock imagery © Getty Images.

All Scripture quotations, unless otherwise indicated, are taken from
the Holy Bible, New International Version®, NIV®. Copyright
©1973, 1978, 1984, 2011 by Biblica, Inc.™ Used by permission of
Zondervan. All rights reserved worldwide. www.zondervan.com The
"NIV" and "New International Version" are trademarks registered in
the United States Patent and Trademark Office by Biblica, Inc.™

Scripture quotations are from New Revised Standard Version Bible,
copyright © 1989 National Council of the Churches of Christ in the United
States of America. Used by permission. All rights reserved worldwide.

ISBN: 978-1-9736-7674-4 (sc)
ISBN: 978-1-9736-7675-1 (e)

Library of Congress Control Number: 2019915606

Print information available on the last page.

WestBow Press rev. date: 10/17/2019

I dedicate this book to my three children, Samantha, Phillip, and Donald, who have been my constant source of love, light, strength, and joy. They are the greatest gift God gave me besides His son.

Preface

My faith journey has been like a meandering stream that has coursed through desert and jungle and arrived in the bright light of God-given freedom through Jesus Christ. This faith, which is the center of my life, has helped me face many challenges: failing marriage, private torment of repressed memories of childhood sexual abuse, depression, divorce, bankruptcy, grief of lost loved ones, physical pain, and loss of a defined purpose and mission. Throughout my faith journey, the Holy Spirit has been guiding and transforming me. The road ahead is not always smooth and has many potholes, but God's love, grace, and mercy are my constant companions.

Over the past 20 years, God has spoken to me in words that I have felt compelled to write. Some were essays, but most took the form of poems. The poems chronicle my faith journey and detail highlights of my path of healing. Some poems sprang spontaneously from my soul; others were the product of prayer and reflection on a certain Bible verse.

In 1994, I started designing my own Christmas cards that included the poems. Each year at the end of summer, I would pray for inspiration and to be shown the message that God wanted me to impart that year. Sometimes it would take months for the message to be revealed. Sometimes it involved research or a particular event in my life, but it usually involved the repetition of a Bible verse that had struck a chord in me. When the time was right, the inspiration would come—sometimes during the night, sometimes while at work, sometimes during a shower, sometimes in the company of friends, sometimes driving to visit family in Pennsylvania—then I would write the poem. It would flow from my brain like magic. When the basic form was there, I would begin to refine it and impose structure and rhythm. My son painted pictures I described to him to capture the illustration that was projected in my mind. The finished poem and painting became the focus of a Christmas card of my own design. When my son moved away, I started painting the illustrations myself.

The illustrations in this book are original paintings by my son or me or original photographs that I took while I was attending Makumira University College in Usa River, Tanzania, and while I was living in Kenya as a volunteer missionary. One photo was taken while I was on a home visit to Pennsylvania.

When I became a member of Via de Cristo, a Lutheran lay movement in the cursillo method, I started making small cards with the poems and paintings to distribute to women on our retreat weekends. The cards were very well received, and I found that the messages in the poems were reaching other women beyond my initial acquaintances. I was amazed by the response. Then my pastor helped me realize that my poetry is my ministry. My greatest desire is that my poems will help other Christians in their healing and their faith journeys, will bring them closer to the triune God, and will help them find the peace that transcends all understanding.

May God bless and keep the reader and bring him or her closer to His side.

Your sister in Christ,
Candy Heinlein

Moonlight on Malindi beach, Kenya. © Candise M. B. Heinlein

Meditations on Om
cmb heinlein

Like the rising and setting of the sun,
Like the waxing and waning of the moon,
Like the ebbing and flowing of the sea,
Like the earth's ever-changing seasons,
I have a rhythm.

God infused me with the same energy He infused all of nature—
We are one in Him.

As in the chokecherries upon which the birds feed in winter
Or the salmonberry, the Athabascan arctic orange,
There is harmony in God's creation, a rhyme and a reason.
I have harmony, a rhyme and a reason.

I reach to touch the edge of His cloak,
He turns, smiles, and says,
"Daughter, your faith has healed you.
Go and be healed of your disease."
And I am healed.

Then the woman, seeing that she could not go unnoticed, came trembling and fell at his feet. In the presence of all the people, she told why she had touched him and how she had been instantly healed. Luke 8:47

Autumn-painted hillsides. © 2004 *Phillip C. Heinlein*

Gifts

cmb heinlein

As you survey the brightly packaged gifts
Of love beneath your Christmas tree,
Squint, use your mind's eye, and behold
Those sent by God to thee.

There is the shimmering gold and diamond
Of sun-filled, dew-dropped summer's morn;
The true blue of a loyal friend;
The velvet, child newborn.

The Autumn-painted hillsides are deftly
Wrapped in a patchwork quilt design;
Ardent lovers, fiery red;
Marital bliss, old wine.

In iridescent white and silver lace,
Lie winter's hoarfrost, ice, and snow;
Bells bedeck childhood's tinkling laugh;
Jewels box wisdom's glow.

There are some, however, whose somber hues
Their inherent value forsake;
Black of illness, handicap, pain,
As gift is hard to take.

But let us remember the greatest gift
Yet sent us (God's son once born,
Died for us) was ghastly wrapped in
Nails, blood, and crown of thorn.

And perhaps what we once perceived as loss
Will become seen as only dross;
Pain, the fire of refining gold
From impure ore of old.

So let us rejoice, give thanks, for all God's
Gifts, the splendid and the concealed,
For He who was born on Christmas day,
Our lives has richly filled.

He will sit as a refiner and purifier of silver; he will purify the Levites and refine them like gold and silver. Malachi 3:3

Pasture with daffodils. © 2004 Phillip C. Heinlein

Joy
cmb heinlein

My heart spills forth with a bubbling tide
That quenches all thirst, refreshes all weariness,
And invigorates all senses; for, I have
Joy in the Lord.

My soul soars with an ethereal vapor
That races with birds, dances with sunshine,
And frolics with daffodils; for, I have
Joy in the Lord.

My body explodes with an electrified sensation
That intensifies creation's palette, embosses creation's
Textile, and amplifies creation's chorus; for, I have
Joy in the Lord.

My mind reposes with an eternal peace
That knows His love, accepts His forgiveness,
And seeks His pleasure; for, I have
Joy in the Lord.

With joy you will draw water from the wells of salvation. Isaiah 12:3

Oil lamp. © 2004 Phillip C. Heinlein

The Lamp
cmb heinlein

Hollow me out, oh Lord.
Remove the muck and mire,
Uproot the seeds of evil.
Scrape away the tarnish of selfishness.
Scrub and polish my interior, then
Pour into me the fragrant oil of Your
Love, wisdom, forgiveness, and goodness.
Trim my wick and
Ignite me with Your Spirit that
Your light may shine brightly in a
World of darkness and despair.

In the same way, let your light shine before men, that they may see your good deeds and praise your Father in heaven. Matthew 5:16

Ox-drawn plow. © 2004 Phillip C. Heinlein

Rest for My Soul
cmb heinlein

Living, giving, reaping, weeping,
Feeling, reeling, caring, bearing,
Hoping, coping, striving, thriving,
Dying, sighing, leaving, grieving.
I am battle weary, Lord.
My heart is numb
And my body lethargic.
My soul cries, "Rest!"
I take Your yoke upon me
And learn from You;
For You are gentle
And humble of heart,
And with You I will find
Rest for my soul.

Come to me, all you who are weary and burdened, and I will give you rest. Take my yoke upon you and learn from me, for I am gentle and humble in heart, and you will find rest for your souls. Matthew 11:28–29

Painting of Bethlehem star. © 1999 Phillip C. Heinlein

Waiting for the Redemption
cmb heinlein

Sometimes we just have to fall,
So we can learn to walk tall.
God, loving parent, allows us to stray,
Knowing we will learn a lesson that way.
He will guide, comfort us, and ease the dread
As we navigate rough seas of the dead—
Friendship, love, trust, large pieces of ourselves,
Employment, good health, pieces of others' selves.
Each part of a life that will be no more.
Fear not! He placed a beacon on the shore.
It is a cross-shaped star above a child,
Who is humble, innocent, meek, and mild.
So if we stay focused on that same star,
Redemption will come, be it near or far.
Sometimes we just have to fall,
So we can learn to walk tall.

Do not let your hearts be troubled. Trust in God; trust also in me.
John 14:1

Sun breaking through clouds. © 2004 Phillip C. Heinlein

The Good Addiction
cmb heinlein

My name is Candy, and I am an addict.
My addiction is the focus of my life.
It affects every relationship *in* my life—
The man on the street, my coworkers, the checkout girl at the grocery store,
My husband, my children, casual acquaintances, and my closest friends.
I crave the clarity of mind, the calm, and the peace that
Comes from my addiction.
I love the giddiness and utter joy that it brings.
I marvel at the endurance and intensity of each dose,
And love to share my addiction with others.
I am committed to the recruitment of new addicts,
The younger the better.
With complete awareness, I surrender my entire life to my addiction.
I am in no need of a 12-step program or a detoxification clinic;
For my addiction is my cure.
I am addicted to God's love.

Whoever does not love does not know God, because God is love.
1 John 4:8

Desert well. © 2004 Phillip C. Heinlein

The Road to Nineveh
cmb heinlein

Lord, there are so many parched souls searching for the oasis of living water.
They need a guide through the desert; someone to bring them to you, Father.
You ask, "Whom shall I send?" With one breath I ask, "Is it I?"
With the next breath, I begin to list a multitude of reasons why
I am not worthy or good enough to undertake what you ask.
I am not wise enough, free enough, nor strong enough for this task.
I do not want to go to Nineveh, and so the whale swallows me I fear.
And I dwell in darkness for days, weeks, months, and even years.
I pray for rescue from my dark captivity so I can see the light once more.
So through your grace I emerge, wiser, stronger, and somewhat pure.
I stand drenched in Your light, feast on Your life-giving bread,
And feel the well within me team with life that is Spirit fed.
"Now go to Nineveh," You say. "But what if my bread becomes stale,
And my well runs dry?" I complain. "You needn't worry about your well.
The water I give is a spring that wells up to eternal life," You reply.
"My living bread is given daily; you only need ask for a new supply.
So do not be afraid. Share them freely and generously;
For, it is through sharing these gifts that you become closer to me."
And so, Lord, here I am. Mold me, teach me, and prepare me
For the road to Nineveh; for, side by side we'll make the journey.

Then Jesus declared, "I am the bread of life. He who comes to me will never go hungry, and he who believes in me will never be thirsty." John 6:35
Whoever believes in me, as the Scripture has said, streams of living water will flow within him. John 7:38

Celebration of Christ's birth. © 2001 Phillip C. Heinlein

Enjoy the Ride!
cmb heinlein

Life is like riding on a Greyhound bus.
The driver has the map and knows the route;
Experience and knowledge gain our trust.
He is a symbol of authority,
And we as passengers surrender ours.
Our destiny's secure; he has the fee.
If we should try to overtake his role,
We could get lost, break down, or arrive late,
Get stuck in a rut, hit a deep pothole.
But when we sit back and enjoy the ride,
Allow the driver to take full control,
Even a detour can be a scenic surprise.
So run our lives when God is in control.
All curves are safe, each detour's exciting.
We are worry free! Christ paid our toll.
So relax and celebrate your freedom.
He knew you in the womb and made your map.
Go God, and then leave the driving to Him.

*Before I formed you in the womb I knew you, before you were born I
set you apart; I appointed you as a prophet to the nations. Jeremiah 1:5*

Winter scene. © 2004 Candise M. B. Heinlein

Be Still

cmb heinlein

Before I knew Your unfathomable peace,
Before my mind, body, and soul were at ease,
I didn't know how to just sit and to be,
Thought I had to constantly do to be me.
Isn't that how success is measured on earth?
Don't our activities determine our worth?
Sew, cook, bake, clean, aerobicize, earn money,
Sing, play bells, teach, tend altar, be a mommy.
But all this commotion causes too much noise
And drowns out the quiet whisper of Your voice.
So now I am still; I sit, listen, and learn,
Your approval the only one I need earn.
For You measure success by what's in my heart
And by the way that I am doing my part
To tell the world about Your abundant love,
Sharing with all the light that comes from above.

*Be still, and know that I am God; I will be exalted among the nations,
I will be exalted in the earth. Psalm 46:10*

Seekers running to the stable. © 2003 Phillip C. Heinlein

Draw Near
cmb heinlein

God could have clipped our wings,
And like parrots we could sit
On His shoulders and sing
Offerings from His Holy writ.

But parrots don't understand
What they say and have no choice
But to stay close at hand,
Mocking their master's voice.

So God gave us the freedom to choose
The safe and warm place at His side.
And when He fears our love to lose,
He actively pursues us worldwide.

We can be like a runaway dog,
Panting with no destination or plan
Till we drop at His feet like a log
Exhausted, our course already ran.

Or we can be like a stubborn kite
Caught in the wind of ambition,
Breaking our string and leaving His sight,
Only to be tangled in the tree of temptation.

Like Tom Hanks's Wilson, adrift on the tide,
We can move farther away with each wave;
By refusing to use appendages at each side,
Laziness keeps us from Him who would save.

So you see; it all comes down to choice.
God is always trying to draw near to us;
We meet by choosing to run toward His voice.

Draw near to God and He will draw near to you. James 3:8a

23

Winter bird and berries. © 2004 Phillip C. Heinlein

Hope Springs Eternal
cmb heinlein

As you spend your forty days in the sand
Waiting for God to lead you into the Promised Land,
Remember to trust in Him; for, He is faithful,
And you will find endless blessings for which to be grateful.
You see this desert is your proving ground,
Where lessons are learned and insights abound.
Through the hardened hearts of men
And Satan's set backs again and again,
God will prove His power and sovereignty
And unto Him the glory will be.
So learn from the bird waiting for spring
And the abundance of food it will bring.
The bird does not fret, nor does it worry;
For, its manna is the tree's dried berry.
No matter what season, weather, or tide,
Our Lord God will always provide.

Anyone who trusts in Him will never be disappointed. Romans 9:33

Snowflakes seen through a window. © 2005 Candise M. B. Heinlein

God's Sonnet
cmb heinlein

Behold, for I am one of God's amazing works of art,
With His prodigious love, He has created every part.
When I was in the womb, He knitted each DNA strand,
And He drew every inch of me in His very fine hand.
Then He wrote a sonnet more ingenious than Shakespeare's:
My entire life staged in seconds, minutes, hours, days, and years.
Each line is a thread weaving together my existence,
Linking my sonnet to your sonnet with God's holy presence.
But my sonnet is mine alone, unique as a snowflake.
It illustrates my every talent, flaw, joy, and heartache.
It maps the very second that Christ and I became one,
And how my works would glorify God through Jesus Christ,
His son.
So I yield to the Holy Spirit and wait for the times
When God will miraculously reveal how my next line rhymes.

We are God's workmanship, created in Christ Jesus to do good works,
which God prepared in advance for us to do. Ephesians 2:8

Abyss unknown. © 2006 Candise M. B. Heinlein

Where Are You?

cmb heinlein

Just like a frightened child I huddled
In a dark closet corner in my mind.
As I hid from You, I heard your muffled,
Distant cry, "Where are you?" come from behind
The closet door; stubborn, I clasped my ears
And chose to remain alone with my fears.
And yet, I still prayed for You to help me.
So I opened the door to look outside,
But a fog blocked my path—I could not see.
I would have to leap blindly to Your side!
From the cliff, I leaped the abyss unknown...
And landed on a ledge! Mercy was shown!
Then, slowly I began to understand
That the barriers between me and You
Were built entirely by my own hand.
Tears of joy streamed down my face; for, I knew:
Despite my shame, I shall forever meet
Love, grace, and mercy falling at Your feet.

Then the man and his wife heard the sound of the Lord God as he was walking in the garden in the cool of the day, and they hid from the Lord God among the trees of the garden. But the Lord God called to the man, "Where are you?" Genesis 3:8

Path from chapel, Makumira University College, Usa River, Tanzania. © 2009 Candise M. B. Heinlein

The Race
cmb heinlein

Sometimes I do not know where I am going
As I run this race that is set before me,
But You know the course and through a
Great cloud of witnesses enable me to see.
Dear brother Oswald reminds me that
Because my goings are of You
I can never understand my ways
And must trust and in faith remain true.
When I sink in self-pity over my lot,
The brave Augustana women provide witness
That with You all things are possible
And that You produce more from less.
Beloved sister Gladys stands as a testament
To the power of Your calling and how You use
Lay people to spread Your Word through
Secular tasks and in ways that You choose.
If spiritual darkness tells me I have nothing to offer,
I think of Mother Teresa, the paragon of humble
Service, who despite her own personal darkness
Compelled others to simply "Love your people."
Through this cloud of witnesses,
You have charted the course of the race,
And as always I stand in awe of
Your power, mercy, and grace.

Therefore, since we are surrounded by so great a cloud of witnesses, let us also lay aside every weight and the sin that clings so closely, and let us run with perseverance the race that is set before us. ... Hebrews 12:1–2 [NRSV]

Cloud of witnesses: Oswald Chambers, Gladys Aylward, Augustana Synod female missionaries to Tanganika, and Mother Teresa.

*Cross in compound of Kenya Evangelical Lutheran Church
(KELC), Nairobi, Kenya. © 2010 Candise M. B. Heinlein*

Walking in the Light

cmb heinlein

When I was very young
I loved walking in the light.
Every step was sure
And Your face was always in sight.

Adolescence brought doubt,
And Satan's cold wind snuffed the light
That illumined my path,
Obscuring Your face in the night.

Groping in the darkness,
I could not see rock, rut, or hole
Marring the unknown path,
So stumbling, I would often fall.

Fear pervaded my life
When I had walked in the darkness,
So I rationalized
Those falls and the subsequent mess.

One miraculous day
The Holy Ghost relit my flame;
Your light shone brighter still,
And Your mercy removed my shame.

Now I live in freedom
And security in Your light.
Though my flame may flicker,
Your grace is always in sight.

The people who walked in darkness have seen a great light; those who lived in a land of deep darkness—on them light has shined. Isaiah 9:2 [NRSV]

Baobab trees in Kambu, Kenya. © 2010 Candise M. B. Heinlein

The Simple Heart

cmb heinlein

To thee, LORD, I give my love;
For, You heard my cries and saw my tears.
You looked into the void of my heart
And sent to me Your simple-hearted dove.

When we were low, You saved us
And maintained our faith despite
Our affliction and pain, then rewarded
Our souls with joy bounteous.

To thee, LORD, I give my praise;
For, Your love is steadfast,
And You have blessed my soul;
To You my grateful chorus I raise.

The web of deceit ensnared us;
We felt gutted and dead,
But now we walk in the land of the living,
Our souls free from the chain's rust.

To thee, LORD, I commit body, soul, and mind;
For, You protect the simple heart
And have sent me these wondrous gifts:
A simple-hearted dove and Your love to find.

The LORD protects the simplehearted; when I was in great need, He saved me. Psalm 116:6

*Carved ebony cross being presented to congregation of
Hambal, Tanzania.* © 2009 Candise M. B. Heinlein

Reflections on Ebony Crosses
cmb heinlein

For my beloved KELC brothers and sisters in Christ

Made of contrasting parts
The ebony tree is a metaphor
For the joining of Christian hearts
Within agape communion.

The dark, hard core vibrates
With African energy (drums beating,
Voices singing) and illustrates
The beauty of joy in hardship.

Carved by an artist's hand,
The soft, tan wood has beauty of its own,
But one might think a different land
Produced this light-weight pale trunk.

The wonder of this tree
Is God created dark and light as a
Life form in perfect unity,
Rooted, watered, and fed as one.

Rooted in Christ, watered
By his blood, we are one body in God's
Image that is fed by His Word,
Nurtured by His Holy Spirit.

Without gender or race,
Brother, sister, African, mzungu,*
Work side by side bathed in God's grace,
United by His selfless love.

---

* Swahili for white person.

Crosses of ebony
Show God's hands reaching down to us; a dove,
The Holy Spirit heavenly
Sent to protect, comfort, and guide.

Our hands of black and white
Extend up to God in supplication
While Christ's hands, stretched out left and right,
Join in unity, peace, and love.

There is neither Jew nor Gentile, neither slave nor free, nor is there male and female, for you are all one in Christ Jesus. Galatians 3:28

Waves on Malindi Beach, Kenya. © *2010 Candise M. B. Heinlein*

The Spirit and the Sea
cmb heinlein

I stand by the sea
And ponder how its ebb and flow
Symbolize the Holy Spirit
Washing over me.

Storms stir up the deep
And waves carry foreign treasures.
Some I examine and return,
Some I long to keep.

Life's storms stir my soul,
Exposing rough and well-worn ills,
Depositing new gifts and strengths,
And I am made whole.

Shells wash onto land;
Some are polished, some worn away.
Rocks continuously erode
Into sparkling sand.

Traits caught in the flow
Become honed, transformed, or are lost.
Bad habits gradually grind
Down, leaving a glow.

By force of the sea,
Shorelines are always changing face.
By force of God's grace, the Holy
Spirit changes me.

And all of us with unveiled faces, seeing the glory of the Lord as though reflected in a mirror, are being transformed into the same image from one degree to another; for this comes from the Lord, the Spirit. 2 Corinthians 3:18

Summer cornfields in Pennsylvania. © 2010 Candise M. B. Heinlein

Waiting for the Lord
cmb heinlein

My soul waits in darkness;
My life lies in pieces.
Paralyzed by uncertainty,
My confinement causes distress.

Where are the happy days
Of peace, purpose, mission?
When will I recover the joy
Of walking steadfast in Your ways?

I know the plans You have for me
Are beyond imagination;
Plans not to harm me, but to give me
Hope and future prosperity.

I know my life You hold.
I'm not Humpty Dumpty;
Your hands alone can fit each piece
Of my life back into the mold.

I know You go before
Us to prepare the way.
Land, sea, sky, fish, and plants were first,
Then man, when survival secure.

You know I've not been known
To look before leaping.
This gift of confinement allows
Critical thought, all options shown.

So, Lord, I wait for You
While You prepare the place
That You have planned and prepare me—
Mind, body, soul—to live anew.

Wait for the LORD; be strong and take heart and wait for the LORD.
Psalm 27:14

About the Author

Candise M. B. Heinlein, a former U.S. Air Force (USAF) spouse, is a mother of three grown children with four grandchildren. She graduated Duquesne University in 1979 with a degree in Psychology and then entered the USAF as a munitions maintenance officer. Having left the service when her children were young, she later embarked on a career as an editor of scientific journals. Following her divorce, she felt called to enter seminary and global mission work. She graduated Lutheran Theological Southern Seminary in 2009 with a master's in religion, concentrating in Theology. Her final semester of seminary had been spent at Makumira University College in Usa River, Tanzania, before moving on to a position as a volunteer missionary in the Department of Communications of the Kenya Evangelical Lutheran Church, Nairobi.

In 1991, the author began a healing process that would take her from a victim of childhood sexual abuse to a recovering survivor, and all points in between (i.e., PTSD, depression, anxiety, codependency, marriage counseling, spiritual crises, and divorce). Through it all, God walked with her and whispered in her ear His truths to be shared as poetry. She has found that her poetry is her true ministry.

Printed in the United States
By Bookmasters